I0837560

ANTIFA
BABY'S
ACAB'S

Antifa Baby's ACABs

By Ricky Rat and Garry Goose

Antifa Baby, do you know your ACABs? Check your privilege, please, march together, and sing!
Did you ask for my pronouns? Or will you misgender me, too? Come, little child; I'll deradicalize you.

A is for Anti-racism.
Everyone is a racist, especially you.

C is for Cucks, I mean... polyamory.
Yes, you are totally not a beta
for letting your woman sleep around.
Also, you tested positive for Chlamydia.

A is for Anti-Fascism. It's just an idea. Sort of like your smashed windows and burned car.

B is for Blackness;
celebrate Black History Month with
jazz and spunk,
fried chicken,
watermelon, 
and artificial dehydrated juice packets
(don't sue me, k***-aid.)

D is for Diversity, Neuro-Divergency.

E is for Education,
Educate yourself, your friends,
and your family, and protect
the Environment!

Electric Vehicles are the way to go
(unless you need to travel more than
50 miles).

F is for Fiery but
mostly peaceful protests.

G is for Groomer, a fascist dog whistle

H is for Hanger, to chop up clumps of cells.
Baby, you're a parasite. Stop oppressing your mom.

I is for Inclusion. Let's include everybody except Christians.

J is for Juneteenth. Separate but
Equal to the fourth of July.

This is what Democrats love:

K is for Kindness

K is for Kompassion

K is for Kommunity

L is for Land which was stolen,
and Labor, which is exploitation.

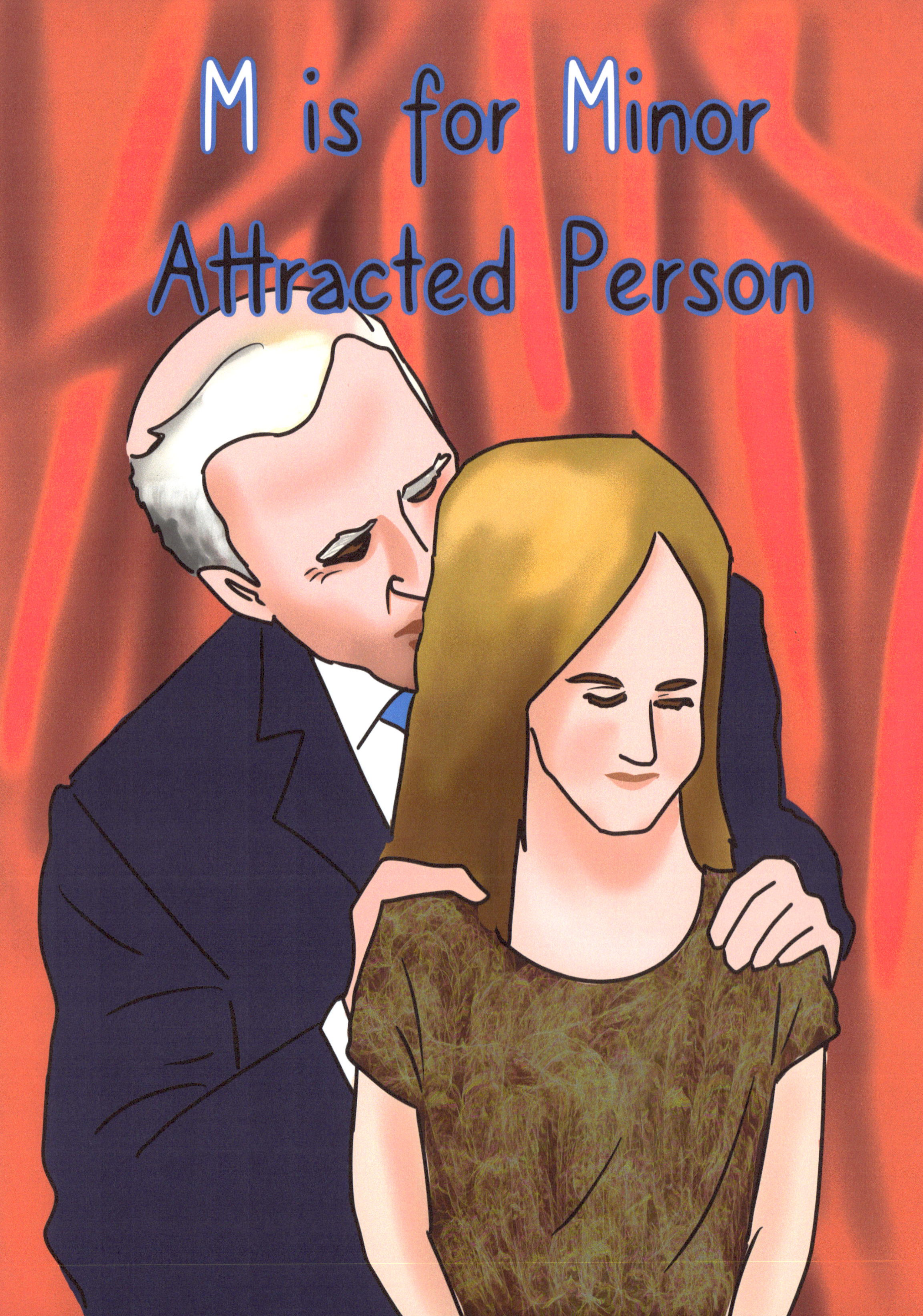

M is for Minor
Attracted Person

N is for the word you cannot say. (you know... what Larry Elder is?)

Okay, fine, I'll say it here. The word is Nazi! Actually, you should say that word, say it to your parents, your teachers, and friends!

O is for Oppression,
O is for Orange!

P is For Pig. Here, take this brick and throw it, kid.

Q ~~anon~~

We won't discuss this letter, The Bidens' Dealings with Burisma, The 2020 Election, Covid's Origins,The Steele Dossier, The Epstein Flight list, or Michael Obama.

R is for Raise your fist in solidarity.

S is for that stuff you find all over San Francisco.

T is for Trans
From the first lady
To the national women's
swimming competition
1
2
3

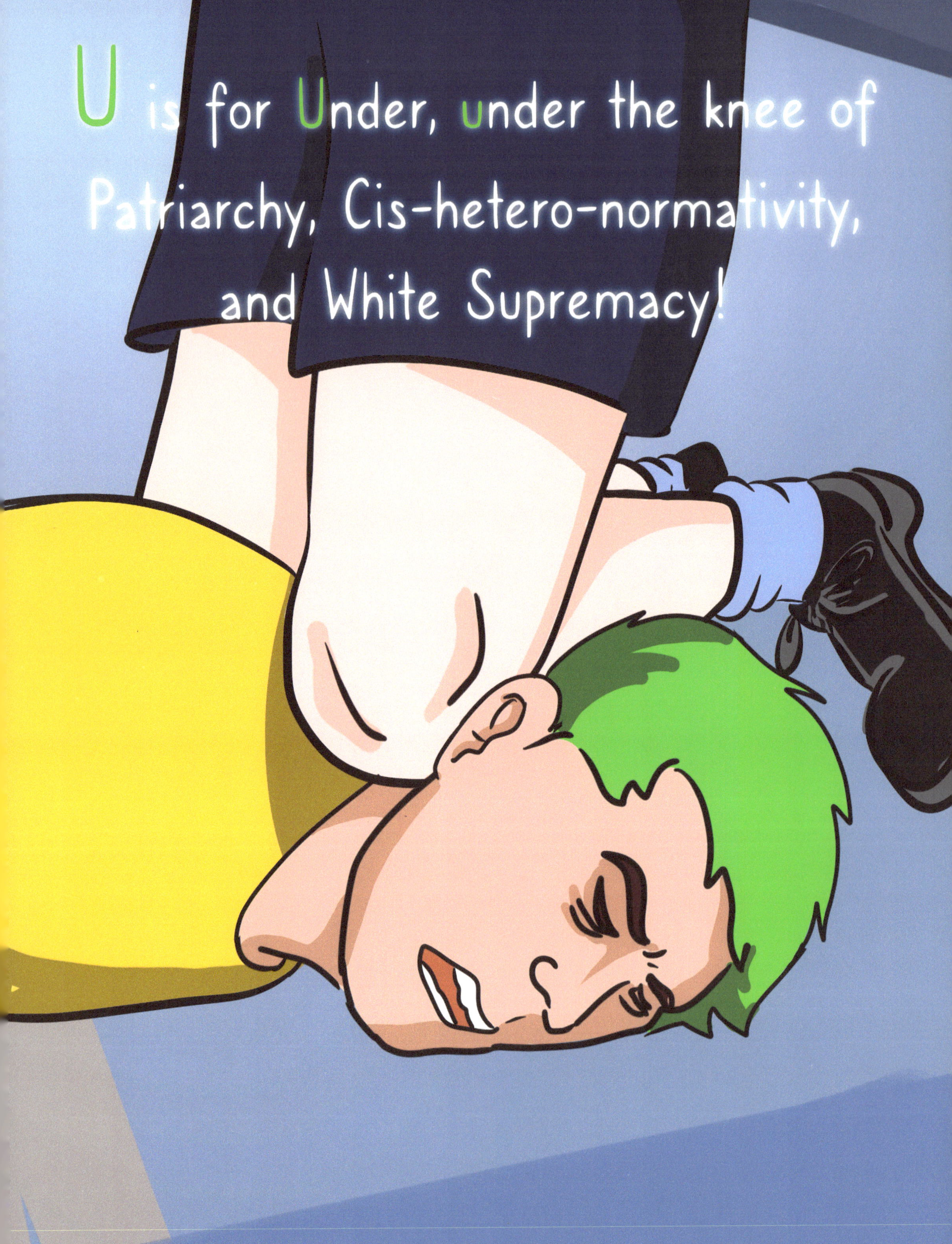
U is for Under, under the knee of Patriarchy, Cis-hetero-normativity, and White Supremacy!

V is for Vaginoplasty. Hey, you want that, right? Quick, before you turn 13!

W is for Whiteness, A cancer of slavery, oppression, and really bland food. And why do you wear sandals to Walmart? WTF man?

X is for Xenophobia. No borders, no walls. Except in our gated communities.

Y is for the chromosome that ruined humanity.

Z is for Zhe and Zher; use
whichever bathroom you please!

Antifa Baby knows his/her/
zhe/zher ACABs; Antifa Baby
sings them with ease.

Now go break some windows, kid.

Follow Ricky Rat Comics on YouTube!

www.ingramcontent.com/pod-product-compliance
Lightning Source LLC
Chambersburg PA
CBHW040207240726
48664CB00002B/866